# Straight Outta Natchez
## "The Story of Black Natchez"
## VOLUME I

Jeremy Houston

## **DEDICATED TO:**
IAN J. HOUSTON &
JEREMIAH R. HOUSTON

# TABLE OF CONTENTS

# INTRODUCTION

In the 300 years of the city of Natchez's existence.
There are not many places in the United States that
can live up to the majesty of Natchez, Mississippi.
Established as a French settlement in 1716.
Members of the Bambara Nation were the first
enslaved Africans to come to Natchez. The Bambara
were known for their cultivation skills. With those
skills, they would go to contribute with the
economic success of the European settlers. In 1729,
members of the Bambara Nation along with the
Natchez Nation (the original inhabitants) attacked
the French at Fort Rosalie. This event became
known as the "Natchez Massacre." Although they
were overtaken with the Natchez Nation by French,
the presence of the African was etched into the
culture of Natchez forever. In the following years to
come more and more enslaved Africans came to the
Natchez region. Sixty years later, Abdul Rahman
Ibrahim Ibn Sori, a prince from the Fulani Nation in
West Africa, was enslaved for forty years in Natchez.
Through it all Abdul Rahman Ibrahim never gave up
hope. Dr. John Cox, an Irish surgeon, was in
Natchez and recognized Abdul Rahman Ibrahim at a
market place selling food. Cox approached Thomas
Foster (the man who was Abdul Rahman Ibrahim
owner in Natchez) to purchase Abdul Rahman
Ibrahim's freedom but Foster refused.  Dr. Cox, to
no avail, continued the cause for Ibrahim's freedom
until his death. Abdul Rahman Ibrahim would

eventually gain his and his wife Isabella's freedom after the Sultan of Morocco wrote a letter to United States President John Quincy Adams. Foster freed Abdul Rahman Ibrahim but the conditions of his freed were, Ibrahim and his family could not enjoy the freedoms of a free man in the United States.Also he and Isabella had to leave the country and migrate back to Africa. Abdul Rahman Ibrahim would go on to travel the country on speaking engagements to raise funds for their migration back to Africa. He would raise enough money to purchase the freedoms of two of his children and their families. Eventually, Abdul Rahman Ibrahim successfully made it to the west coast (Liberia) of Africa but died before making it to his native land.

Meanwhile in Natchez, the increase in cotton production in the region caused planters in the region to increase their enslaved population. At one time, the sale of enslaved people of African descent in Natchez was so common, that they were sold on almost every street corner in the city of Natchez. With outbreak of Cholera in Natchez, city officials decided to designate a specific area outside the city limits for the sale of the enslaved people of African descent. This area was and is today known as the Forks of the Road. Built around April 1833, some sources say that over 2,000 enslaved people African descent were sold yearly from 1833 to 1863 at the Forks of the Road. "No one knows exactly how many of our ancestors were exactly sold at the Forks of the Road," says Ser Seshs Ab Heter-Boxley.

Enslave traders like Isaac Franklin and John
Armfield of 1315 Duke Street Alexandria, Virginia
sold and transported our ancestors of African
descent to the Forks of the Road Slave Market for
many years. Also in the vicinity of the Forks of
Roads were enslave dealers like John James,
Blackwell and Murphy, and R.H. Elam were some of
the many enslave traders to sell people of African
descent in Natchez and the surrounding areas.In July
1863, the Forks of the Road ceased operations as a
slave market in Natchez. The Forks of the Road
became the recruitment center of the Union Army
for the newly emancipated slaves of African descent.
The holding pens or cells used to incarcerate the
enslaved torn down.
The wood of the old pens or cells were used to
construct a barracks for the newly formed USCT
(United States Colored Troops) Individuals like
Wilson Brown, who emancipated himself during the
Civil War, saw the USS Hartford floating down the
Mississippi River near Natchez. Brown jumped and
swam in the Mississippi aboard the USS Hartford.
Brown was awarded the Medal of Honor for his
actions at the Battle of Mobile Bay in 1864. The
period after the Civil War was known as
Reconstruction. Reconstruction was instrumental in
the federal government setting conditions that would
allow the rebellious Southern states back into the
Union. Natchez proved to be the model for political,

economic, and social success for the newly emancipated black people during Reconstruction. During Reconstruction, Natchez had a black mayor (Robert Wood) black United States Congressman (John R. Lynch) and a black United States Senator (Hiram R. Revels). Also Natchez had an integrated school board and board of Alderman. There where black lawyers, doctors, and black sheriffs (Louis Winston and William McCary). There aren't many places in America that claim hold to that success. After Reconstruction, "Jim Crow" laws came into full effect across the south, especially in Natchez. In the 1920's, the Universal Negro Improvement Association African Communities League (UNIA-ACL) a group led by the Honorable Marcus Mosiah Garvey, came into existence in Natchez.Local minister R.H. Cosgrove led the UNIA in Natchez. In 1924, Cosgrove reported at an international convention of the UNIA that "he pastored a little church of 500 members, and everyone was a member of the association, as he was of the opinion that he was to be a spiritual leader he should also be able to lead in temporal affairs." Cosgrove attended the convention to see himself so that he could bring back a true friend report to the people in Natchez who trusted in him. The UNIA continued to have a presence in Natchez until the 1940's. On April 23,

1940, the Rhythm Club Fire took the lives of 209 black residents of Natchez. Walter Barnes and his Royal Creolians orchestra came to Natchez to perform before traveling home to Chicago, Illinois. Barnes, along with some of his orchestra perished in the fire that night. Individuals from Natchez like Woodrick McGuire, band director at Brumfield High School and Clarence "Bud" Scott Jr., son of the late Natchez jazz musician Clarence "Bud" Scott Sr, perished in the fire too. In the aftermath of the Rhythm Club Fire, fire codes for buildings across the country were established because of the fire. The Rhythm Club Fire has been memorialized in songs such as "Mississippi Fire Blues" and "Natchez Mississippi Blues" by the Lewis Bronzeville Five; "The Death of Walter Barnes" by Leonard Caston; "The Natchez Burnin" by Howlin' Wolf; and "Natchez Fire" by John Lee Hooker. The Civil Rights Movement of the 1960's was a very intense time for Natchez and Adams County. Natchez Activist William "Bill" Ware was the first person to be arrested for civil rights in Natchez. Ware was instrumental in groups like Student Non Violent Coordinating Committee (SNCC) and the Mississippi Freedom Party (MFD) coming to help with the movement in Natchez. In August 1965, George Metcalfe was bombed in his vehicle at

Armstrong Rubber and Tire Plant. Shock waves went throughout the community after the bombing of Metcalfe. Individuals like Rev. James Stokes, Otis Fleming, Richard Lewis, and James Jackson organized the Deacons for the Defense and Justice in response to the bombing of Metcalfe and to combat the Ku Klux Klan in Natchez. Charles Evers (brother of Mississippi Field Secretary, the late Medgar Evers) mobilized the NAACP to Natchez after the bombing of Metcalfe. Evers along with other representatives of the community presented the city of Natchez with a list of demands for equal treatment in Natchez. In October 1965, over 200 black people were arrested and sent Mississippi State Penitentiary (Parchman), for Parading Without Permit. This in return led to one of the most successful economic boycotts during the civil rights movement in Natchez. The black residents economically boycotted every white business in Natchez and Adams County. The boycott of white businesses by black people in Natchez and Adams County hit white businesses hard. Whites in Natchez begged and pleaded with blacks in the area to shop at their stores. This was in due part so white businesses wouldn't lose money for Christmas. In 1966, Ben Chester White who had nothing to do with the civil rights movement, was killed but the Ku

Klux Klan in Adams County. The Klansmen hoped that by killing White they could lure Dr.Martin Luther King Jr. to Natchez and kill him, too. Justice for Ben Chester White came for in 2003. Ernest Avants was convicted and sentenced to life in prison for the murder of Ben Chester White. In June 1968, racial tensions came to a head in Natchez. After the shooting of a black man by a white man on the corner of Pine Street (now Martin Luther King Jr. Street) and St Catherine Street.  A riot broke out in downtown Natchez. The National Guard had to take control of Natchez. The black organizations of Natchez refused to meet with the mayor at the time John J. Nossier. After the riot of 1968, Natchez began the process of racial reconciliation. Barney Scobey Sr., Phillip West, and George F. West Sr. were some of the first blacks since Reconstruction to hold political office in Natchez and Adams County. In the late 1980s, Natchez High School came into existence in the city of Natchez. This was in due part to the Brown V. Board of Education 1954 decision that ruled school segregation was illegal. Thirty years after the Brown V. Board decision, Natchez and Adams County finally desegregated public schools in the area.  As a result of the desegregation of public schools in Natchez, the author of this book and countless others from Natchez have had the opportunity to attend integrated schools in Natchez. It was at Natchez High, teachers like Mrs. Francis Doss, Mrs. Alexine P. Wright, Mrs. Susan Freeney, Coach Mike Martin, Mr. Cleveland Moore Jr., and Mr. Joe D. Wallace inspired myself to strive for a better quality of life in Natchez.

# CHAPTER 1
# ELIZABETH TAYLOR GREENFIELD

During the twentieth century, singers like Marion Anderson and Leontyne Price, wowed many people around the world with their gift of singing. Elizabeth Taylor Greenfield in the nineteenth century would build the foundation to what Anderson and Price would accomplish in the twentieth century. Born a slave in 1819 in Natchez, Mississippi, as Elizabeth Taylor. As an infant, Elizabeth and her family were emancipated by their owner, Elizabeth Greenfield, a Quaker from Philadelphia, Pennsylvania. Thus far she would known for the rest of her life as Elizabeth Taylor Greenfield. While Elizabeth was an infant, Mrs. Greenfield would move her and Elizabeth to Philadelphia, Pennsylvania. As a youth, Elizabeth was a self-taught vocalist and musician, who often provided entertainment for her mistress and the mistresses guests. After the death of her mistress, Elizabeth supported herself by performing public and private concerts. It was also during this time she became known as "The Black Swan."

On March 31, 1853, Elizabeth Taylor Greenfield "The Black Swan" made her New York City debut at Metropolitan Hall, to a crowd over 4,000 people. Later that year, Elizabeth would go on to travel to Europe for concert engagements in Scotland, England, and Ireland. While in London, England, she would find herself in an unfortunate circumstance. Elizabeth's manager abandoned and left her penniless. Feeling hopeless and distraught, Elizabeth arranged to meet Uncle Tom's Cabin author Harriet Beecher

Stowe. With the help of Stowe, Elizabeth performed before English gentry or people high social class. This would lead to her performing in Buckingham Palace in a command performance before Queen Victoria. Upon her return to the United States, Elizabeth was not celebrated for her performance before Queen Victoria. Though Elizabeth had a strong white audience, Fredrick Douglass, a well known orator and abolitionist said of Elizabeth, "We marvel that Miss Greenfield can allow herself to be treated with such palpable disrespect; for the insult is to her, not less than to her race. She must have felt deep humiliation and depression while attempting to sing in the presence of an audience and under arrangements which had thus degraded and dishonored the people to which she belongs. ..She is quite mistaken if she supposes that her success, as an artist depends upon her entire abandonment of self-respect. We warn her also, that this yielding, on her part, to the cowardly and contemptible exactions of the negro haters of this country may meet her in a distant land in a manner which she little imagines." This was especially true, when she was refused entrance to a university music class because of her race. Determined, Elizabeth opened a music studio in Philadelphia, where she created and directed an opera troupe in the 1860s. During the Civil War, Elizabeth became heavily involved with war relief efforts. She appeared alongside with Fredrick Douglass, Martin Delaney, and Frances E.W. Harper to raise money for various "colored" aged and orphan societies. In the following years of her life, Elizabeth continued to travel the country with her opera troupe fighting racism through their music. On March 31, 1876, Elizabeth Taylor Greenfield died of paralysis in Philadelphia, Pennsylvania. Elizabeth Taylor Greenfield became the first and one of the most celebrated African American singers to gain recognition in both Europe and the United States. With determination, her talents and gifts took her to places beyond what anyone could imagine for a enslaved girl from Mississippi.

# CHAPTER 2
# JOHN ROY LYNCH

During the troublesome days of slavery in America, if you were enslaved, to know how to read and write could get you beaten, sold, mutilated, or even killed. As a might of fact, it was against the law. Individuals like John Roy Lynch defied the system and "stole" an education while being enslaved in Natchez Mississippi. Born on September 10, 1847 on the Tacony Plantation, in Concordia Parish, Louisiana. Lynch's father Patrick Lynch was an Irish born plantation manager and his mother Catherine was a enslaved woman of African descent. After he was born, his father planned to purchase the family's freedom and move them to New Orleans. Before the purchase and move could be finalized, Patrick Lynch died of an illness. Promising to free the family, William Deal, a friend of Patrick, had taken the title of the family from Patrick before he died. But the friend sold the family to Alfred Davis, a planter from the Dunleith Plantation in Natchez, Mississippi. While enslaved at Dunleith, young John worked as a valet for Davis and worked as a house servant for his wife Mrs. Davis. It was during this time that he took every opportunity to to "steal" an education. So whenever there was any education being taught, Lynch eavesdropped on class lessons in the white schools that he worked. In 1863, at the age of sixteen years old, he acquired his freedom through the Union Army's occupation of Natchez. Also during this time Lynch learned photography and managed a successful business in Natchez. From 1868-1869, he was appointed Postmaster and Justice of the Peace by Mississippi Governor Adelbert Ames.As a congressman, he would fight for civil rights and education for newly emancipated blacks in Mississippi. He was instrumental in the first public school for newly emancipated blacks in the city of Natchez—the Union Street School. In 1871, at the age of twenty-four, Lynch was elected Speaker of the Mississippi House of Representatives (making him the only person of African descent to hold this esteemed office in the state's history). Lynch served as a U.S. Congressman from 1869-74 and 1882-83. In 1884, Theodore Roosevelt (who would later become 26th President of the United States) made a moving speech by which he nominated Lynch as Temporary Chairman of the 1884 Republican National Convention in Chicago, Illinois. This made Lynch the person of African descent to chair the convention. He was also the keynote speaker at the convention and the last black keynote speaker until 1968. Also that year, Lynch would marry Ella W. Somerville. They had one child and divorced in 1900. From 1889 to 1893, Lynch was appointed by President Benjamin Harrison to serve as Treasury Auditor of the Navy. In 1898, during the Spanish-American War, Lynch was appointed as a major and paymaster in the Army by President William McKinley. In 1901, Lynch entered the Army as a captain, gaining promotions to major and serving tours of duty in the United States, Cuba, and the Philippines. Lynch retired from the Army in 1911 and moved to Chicago 1912. While in Chicago, Lynch married Cora Williamson, who was twenty seven years younger than he. Admitted to the Chicago bar by reciprocity in 1915, he practiced law for over twenty-five years. During these years he began writing about the Reconstruction period. Lynch published several well-documented works, beginning with The Facts of Reconstruction (1914). He later incorporated a large section of his 1913 history of Reconstruction in his autobiography, Reminiscences of an Active Life, completed shortly before his death in Chicago but not published until 1970, edited by John Hope Franklin. In 1939, Lynch died at the age of 92 in Chicago, Illinois. He was buried with Military Honors in Arlington National Cemetery, due to his entitlement as a Congressman and Veteran.

In Jackson, Mississippi, there's a John R. Lynch Street. In July

2014, Natchez native Jeremy Houston and several residents of Adams County presented a petition to the Adams County Board of Supervisors Change Providence Road in Adams County to John R. Lynch Road. Though the Supervisors didn't change the name of the road, they did name the road John R. Lynch Parkway.

John R. Lynch is a classic example of an individual who overcame a lot of obstacles. From his childhood of slavery to Republican National Chairman, John Roy Lynch become a successful politician, lawyer, author, and African American.

# CHAPTER 3
# HIRAM RHODES REVELS

What if I told you the first person of African descent to become a United States Senator got his political beginnings in Natchez, would you believe me? In the case of Hiram Rhodes Revels Natchez would be the pillar to a lifelong journey through religion and politics.

He was born free in Fayetteville, North Carolina on September 27,1827. Revels was of African and European Ancestry, which classified him as a Mulatto. In 1838, at the age of eleven he was sent to live with his older brother Elias Revels. There Elias gave him an apprenticeship as a barber. In 1841, after the death of his brother Elias, he given his brother's barbershop by his sister-in-law. In 1845, he was ordained a minister in the African Methodist Episcopal Church (A.M.E.). As a young man, he served as minister and teacher throughout the Midwest: in Indiana, Illinois, Ohio, Tennessee, Missouri, and Kansas.

"At times, I was met with a great deal of opposition," said Revels.

In 1854, he was even imprisoned for a short period in Missouri for preaching the gospel to Negroes. After his brief imprisonment, he studied religion at Knox College in Galesburg, Illinois from 1855-57. Upon leaving Knox College, he became a minister at an A.M.E. Church in Baltimore,Maryland. He also took a position as a principal at a black high school in the area. In 1861, the Civil War began. During the war years, Revels served as a Chaplin in the U.S. Army. He recruited and organized black troops in Maryland and Missouri. In 1863, he would come to Mississippi along with regiments of the newly formed United States Colored Troops (U.S.C.T.) to participate in the Battle of VicksburgAfter the war years, Revels relocated his wife Phoebe and family to Natchez. He served as the minister of the Zion Chapel African Methodist Episcopal Church in Natchez. It was in Natchez that Revels began to become more involved in politics. In 1868, during Reconstruction, he was elected the first black Alderman in Natchez.

John Roy Lynch, who was a black congressman from Adams County, later wrote in his book Facts of Reconstruction:
"Revels was comparatively a new man in the community. He had recently been stationed at Natchez as pastor in charge of the A.M.E. Church, and so far as known he had never voted, had never attended a political meeting, and of course, had never made a political speech. But he was a colored man, and presumed to be a Republican, and believed to be a man of ability and considerably above the average in point of intelligence; just the man, it was thought, the Rev. Noah Buchanan would be willing to vote for."

In January 1870, he was invited to give the opening prayer in state legislature.

"That prayer—one of the most impressive and eloquent prayers that had ever been delivered in the [Mississippi] Senate Chamber—made Revels a United States Senator. He made a profound impression upon all who heard him. It impressed those who heard it that Revels was not only a man of great natural ability but that he was also a man of superior attainments," said Congressman John R. Lynch.

Revels was elected by a vote of 81 to 15 to the Mississippi State Senate to finish the term of former president of the Confederacy Jefferson Davis. When he arrived in Washington, D.C., southern Democrats opposed seating him in the Senate. On February 25,1870 became the first place person of African descent to be seated in the United States Senate. Revels' term lasted one year, February 25,1870 to March 3, 1871. In 1871, he resigned with two months left on his term to become President of the first land grant college for Negroes named Alcorn Agricultural and Mechanical College. (now Alcorn State University). He would serve as President of Alcorn twice. He was dismissed from Alcorn during his first term for going against the reelection of Governor Adelbert Ames but was reappointed by the Democratic Party in

1876 until his retirement in 1882. In the latter years of his life, Revels remained active in the Methodist Church. He relocated to Holly Springs, Mississippi and served as an elder in the Upper Mississippi district. He also taught Theology at Shaw College (now Rust College) until his death.

Hiram Revels died on January 16,1901, while attending a conference in Holly Springs, Mississippi. He is buried at Hillcrest Cemetery in Holly Springs, Mississippi. Revels daughter Susan Revels Cayton and her husband Horace Cayton would go on to start a successful black newspaper in Seattle, Washington. Horace Cayton Jr., who was the grandson of Revels, would go to become a prominent American sociologist, newspaper columnist, and author who specialized in studies of working-class black Americans, particularly in mid-20th-century Chicago. Cayton is best remembered as the co-author of a seminal 1945 study of South Side, Chicago: Black Metropolis: A Study of Negro Life in a Northern City.

# CHAPTER 4
# RICHARD NATHAN WRIGHT

During the 20th Century, pioneering African American writer and poet, Richard Wright was born September 4, 1908, in Adams County, Mississippi. Richard's father, Nathaniel Wright's occupation was a share cropper; while his mother Ella Wilson, was a school teacher.

According to Charles Wright (Richard Wright Historian and relative), as a young child, Wright was playing with a box of matches and set the family home a fire. It was one of the worst beatings he would ever receive. Also his father would abandon the family when Wright was five years old. This forced his mother to work domestic jobs away from home from Wright and his brother. The two Wright boys would even spend time in an orphanage for short period. In the early 1920's, his mother became a paralytic. By this time in Wright's life, he and his family had moved from Natchez to Jackson, then to Elaine, Arkansas, and back to Jackson to live with Wright's maternal grandparents. While in Jackson, Wright attended Jim Hill Public School and Smith Robertson Junior High School. At Smith Robertson, Wright was the class valedictorian in 1923. At the age of 15, while in eighth grade, Wright published his first story, "The Voodoo of Hell's Half-Acre." After leaving school, Wright worked a series of odd jobs, and in his free time he delved into American literature. To pursue his literary interests, Wright went as far as to forge notes so he could take out books on a white coworker's library card, as blacks were not allowed to use the public libraries in Memphis. Wright once said "I want my life to count for something." In 1927, Wright left the south and moved to Chicago. Five years later in 1932, Wright became involved with the John Reed Club, an intellectual arm of the Communist party. In 1935, Wright completed his first novel Cesspool. By 1937, Wright moved to New York City, where he forged new ties with Communist Party members. In 1938, Wright also became the Harlem editor of the Daily Worker. That year he also formed a friendship with African American writer Ralph Ellison. After the success of his novel "Uncle Tom's Children" (1938), Wright was finally financially stable to write his next novel "Native Son"(1940). In 1940, with the success of "Native Son"' Wright came back to Natchez to visit his family. Upon arrival, Wright was appalled and shocked to see the conditions blacks were living in Natchez. Wright witnessed residents of Natchez were still trying to cope with loss of 209 African Americans in The Rhythm Night Club. According to Charles Wright, during Wright's visit, he bought his father a pair of dentures. Nathaniel Wright supposedly threw away the dentures in the woods. This would be final time Wright would come to Natchez. According to David Dryer, a local Natchez historian, Wright's inspiration for his novel "The Long Dream" (1958) was in part to what he witnessed following the aftermath of the Rhythm Night Club fire. In 1942, Wright first daughter, Julia Wright, is born on April 15. The F.B.I. also began to investigation on Wright's "12 Million Black Voices" for sedition. In 1945, Wright's novel "Black Boy" is published. Black Boy, a semi autobiography, describes his early childhood in Adams County until his move to Chicago. "Black Boy" successfully appears on the bestsellers list for two months. Mississippi Senator Theodore Bilbo denounced Black Boy as "obscene." In 1946, Wright moved to Paris, France. He would go on to live in France for the rest of his life. While living in France also befriended fellow black writers Chester Himes and James Baldwin. By 1947, Wright became a French citizen. Wright continued traveling throughout Europe, Asia, and Africa. In 1953, Wright traveled to Ghana. During this time, Ghana (known before as the Gold Coast) where Kwame Nkrumah fighting for the country's independence from British. This was inspiration for Wright's nonfiction book "Black Power." In 1955, Wright attended the Bandung Conference. He recorded his observations on the conference as well as on Indonesian cultural conditions in "The Color Curtain: A Report on the Bandung Conference." Upbeat and enthusiastic about the possibilities posed by the conference, Wright gave at least two lectures to Indonesian cultural groups. The last work Wright submitted for publication during his lifetime, The Long Dream, was released in 1958. During the last years of his life, Wright suffered from amoebic dysentery acquired during his travels to Africa or Asia.

Wright's last display of explosive energy occurred on November 8, 1960, in his polemical lecture, "The Situation of the Black Artist and Intellectual in the United States," delivered to students and members of the American Church in Paris. He argued that American society reduced the most militant members of the black community to slaves whenever they wanted to question the racial status quo.

On November 28, 1960, Richard Wright died suddenly of an apparent heart attack while recuperating at the Clinique Eugène Gibez in Paris. He was interred in Le Père Lachaise Cemetery. There have been recurrent rumors that Wright was murdered, but this has not been proven. A number of Wright's works have been published after his death. A collection of Wright's travel writings was published by Mississippi University Press in 2001. Dr. Jerry Ward of Dillard University, co edited the Richard Wright Encyclopedia in 2006.

In 2008, the residents and officials of Natchez and Adams County honored Richard Wright by naming a portion of US Highway 84, Richard Wright Memorial Highway

# CHAPTER 5
# WHARLEST JACKSON SR.

During the three hundred years of the city of Natchez's existence, there have been many who have stood tall against economical oppression and racism. Wharlest Jackson Sr. was and today still stands as a pillar of hope for the past, present, and future of African Americans in Natchez, Mississippi. Born December 7, 1930 in DeLeon, Florida. Jackson's father, who also was a minister, reared Wharlest in an ethical and religious family. As a young adult, Jackson enlisted in the United States Army. While enlisted, he would go on to serve in the Korean War. In 1954 Jackson married a woman named Exerlena, whom he met two years before in Chicago. They decided to move and start a family in Natchez, Mississippi. To their union, came four daughters and one son. Jackson being the primary bread winner, worked at Armstrong Rubber Company. While employed at Armstrong, Jackson became friends with George Metcalfe. Jackson and Metcalfe's relationship would grow to one as "blood brothers" in the remaining years of Jackson's life. While employed at Armstrong, Metcalfe led efforts to open higher paying positions to blacks who worked within the factory. Jackson even took on the position of Treasure of the NAACP's Natchez chapter. On August 27, 1965, Metcalfe now president of the NAACP's Natchez chapter, car was bombed at Armstrong Rubber Company. Metcalfe survived but was seriously injured. With Jackson's help, Metcalfe recovered and returned to Armstrong for work. Following the return of Metcalfe, Jackson took on a seventeen cent promotion as a chemical mixer, which had previously been held by white men. This put a large target on Jackson's back. Metcalfe even advised Jackson to start checking his hood before starting his vehicle. The two of them also began riding to work together. On February 27, 1967, which was Jackson's first day as a chemical mixer, Jackson worked his shift at Armstrong with no problem. Jackson even attained overtime hours that day. Soon after 8 p.m., he got in his pickup truck and headed toward home in a cold rain. As Jackson traveled down Minor Street, a bomb detonated, when he used his turn blinker. The bomb destroyed his vehicle and left him fatally wounded. The Natchez community was shocked and surprised at the bombing. Governor Paul Johnson called Jackson's murder "an act of savagery which stains the honor of our state." Charles Evers and the Natchez NAACP organized a protest, leading 2,000 demonstrators to watch the changing of the shift at the Armstrong plant. From the Armstrong plant, the demonstrators marched to the place where Jackson died, and then to Rosehill Baptist Church, where they had an hour-long meeting. Following Jackson's death, the FBI launched an intensive probe that it quickly expanded to include other Klan-related murders and crimes. Investigators speculated that Jackson was a victim of the Silver Dollar Group, a violent, heavily armed cell of the Ku Klux Klan. More than 40 years after the murder, the Wharlest Jackson case is still open and no arrests have been made. As of May 2010, the case appeared on the FBI Cold Case List. In August 2010, Wharlest Jackson's family met its fundraising goal for a commemorative marker to place at the site of his death. Roy Wilkins quoted,"Wharlest Jackson had begun to climb out of the darkness into the light and for this he was cut down." This may be true but the same values and work ethic, Wharlest Jackson Sr. exemplified is still living through individuals in Natchez and the United States. On February 27, 2016, fourty-nine years to the date of his death, local Natchez based, Miss Lou Heritage Group & Tours dedicated a community garden in the community of Minorville to the legacy of Wharlest Jackson Sr. Those in attendance were family members like his son Wharlest Jackson Jr. and daughter Denise J. Ford. Wharlest Jackson Jr. quoted, "My family is grateful and thankful to see people honor our father for the contributions he made to this community."

# CHAPTER 6
# PHILLIP WEST

In the 1960's, if someone would have asked Phillip West if he would become the first black man to hold the job of mayor in Natchez since Reconstruction, looks of confusion would have been your answer. "I couldn't have imagined being mayor as a young person, I didn't know where city hall was," said West.

Decades later, not only would he know where city hall was, it became the place where Phillip West served Natchez as it mayor from 2004-08. Born November 30, 1946 in Natchez Mississippi. West was the seventh of twelve children to the late Samuel and Elodie West. West and his siblings grew up on Vinier Street, a part of the city where all he had to do was look out his front door to be reminded that segregation was in full force. As a youth, West interests were as many young men, girls and sports. But the young West also had an interest in government. While a student at Sadie V.Thompson High School, West recalls Ms. Eva Brown, his government/history instructor, as someone who sparked his interest in government. "She (Eva Brown) was an inspiring teacher. I gave her an 8x10 graduation picture. Which was a big thing at that time," said West. In 1964, he graduated from Sadie V. Thompson High School. Upon graduation, West left Natchez to find work in the northern states. Though being able to find work in the north, West decided he needed to come back to Natchez. By January 1965, West enrolled as a student at Alcorn A&M College (now Alcorn State University). On the day prior to his enrollment at Alcorn, West and his father had an encounter with the KKK (Ku Klux Klan) in Adams and Franklin Counties. "The most chilling words to me that my father uttered … during the course of this was, 'Philip, if they've got the road blocked, all I can tell you to do is close your eyes,'" West recalled. West who was only nineteen years old at the time, life was changed forever.As a student at Alcorn, West was the Co-Captain of the Baseball team. West also became a student activist. While at Alcorn, during a protest march being held on the Lorman campus, Mississippi state troopers sprayed tear gas and shot rubber bullets into certain dormitories on the campus to subdue the protest. West attended Alcorn from 1965-1968. In 1969, West was drafted by the United States Army. West was medically discharged from the Army after three months of service. West returned to Natchez and became totally involved in matters concerning the betterment of his community. He served as Vice President of the Natchez NAACP from 1972-1974 and President of the Natchez NAACP from 1974-1980. . It was during this time, West chaired the "Black Committee on Higher Education for Natchez Adams County." Originally, the committee organized to locate a branch of the University of Southern Mississippi in Adams County. This led to a decision by the Federal District Court ruling Natchez Adams County was the territorial rights Alcorn State University. In 1980, West was elected to the Adams County Board of Supervisors. He along with Barney Scoby Sr. were two of the first blacks to hold the positions of supervisor in Adams County. West served as supervisor in Adams County until 1997. In 1997, he was elected to the Mississippi House of Representatives. During that period, West served as chairman of the Mississippi Legislative Black Caucus for two terms.

   In 1996, West was defeated by incumbent Larry "Butch" Brown. According to West, he ran to make a point that things weren't being run the way he thought they should. "In 1996, I ran against "Butch" as a protest candidate. I decided to run to show people that there were other important issues we needed to focus on in the city of Natchez," said West. Eight years later in 2004 defied the odds and was elected the first black mayor of Natchez since Reconstruction. West was quoted as saying "I was shocked. I knew if I didn't win the black community would be hurt. It was by the grace of God that I won."As mayor, West's goals were to lift the spirits of a long suffering city. Some of West accomplishments as mayor of Natchez were:

-The development of Magnolia Bluffs Casino and the Natchez Grand Hotel in the city of Natchez.

-The highest sales tax revenue in the city's history was under West's administration.

-The Natchez Walking Trails Project was started under West's administration.

-Crime in the city of Natchez went down under West's administration

-African American sites like the Forks of the Road Slaves Market Historic Site was brought to the forefront in the tourism industry in Natchez.

In 2008, West lost his re-election bid to Jake Middleton. But what hurt West more than losing the election to Middleton was the death of his wife. "My wife died about 9 months before my bid for re- election. It was a very trying and hurtful time," said West.

In 2012, West ran for mayor of Natchez again. West vowed to finish what he started eight years earlier as mayor. "I felt like we needed to focus on economic development in the city of Natchez. That's was why I ran for mayor of Natchez in 2012," said West.

Though he lost Larry "Butch" Brown again, residents of Natchez still are asking West to run for mayor. "I'm not going run anymore. I can still be effective and be a help to Natchez even without being mayor," said West.

# ABOUT THE AUTHOR

Jeremy Houston is the grandson of Freeman and Esther Reason and son of Alvin and Theresa Houston. Jeremy was born on December 25, 1987, in Natchez,Mississippi. He was reared at a young age by his parents, grandparents, close relatives, and the communityof Minorville. Jeremy is the father of Ian Josiah Houston. He graduated from Natchez High School in 2006. Upon graduation, he attended Northeast Mississippi Community College on a basketball scholarship. After one season in college, he decided to join the United States Marine Corps. While  in the Marines, he deployed to Afghanistan, Japan, Thailand, Kenya and countless other locations on the globe. Also,  it was there where he was able to play organized basketball in across the United States and the world.

After five years of service to the Marines, He moved back to Natchez in 2012. Immediately, he connected with Ser -BOXLEY and Darrell White tobegan working on the Equalization of Natchez History concerning people or African descent or black people in Natchez and the surrounding areas. Groups like the National Black United Front, New Black Panther Party, National of Islam under the Honorable Louis Farrakhan, and the Ethiopian World Federation are some of the national groups that have worked with him and others in Natchez. Locally, he is a member of the Miss Lou Heritage Group & Tours, and the Friends of the Forks of the Road Society.

In 2013 he volunteered for the late Chokwe Lumumba's mayoral campaign in Jackson, Mississippi. He followed that with volunteering for Chokwe Antar Lumumba 's mayoral campaign in 2014.Jeremy is also an advocate for Cannabis laws being amended or changed in the state of Mississippi. This is in due part to the "Public School to Prison" pipeline. In 2016, Jeremy Houston ran for Alderman of Ward 4 in Natchez. His campaign motto was

"ONE WARD! ONE AIM! ONE DESTINY! Also that year, the Miss Lou Heritage Group & Tours LLC was established by Houston. The Miss Lou Heritage Group & Tours is a tour company dedicated to upkeeping and uplifting the stories of African American in the Mississippi Louisiana lower valley region.

Jeremy is committed to the success of Natchez "By Any Means Necessary." "When we all wake up and realize that we must put aside our petty differences and learn to agree to disagree on small matters. We will go to a level Natchez has never seen before."- Jeremy Houston

# SOURCES/REFERENCES

## JOHN ROY LYNCH

http://history.house.gov/People/Detail/17259

http://www.blackpast.org/aah/lynch-john-roy-1847-1939

Reminiscences of an Active Life: The Autobiography of John Roy Lynch by John R. Lynch and John Hope Franklin

The Facts of Reconstruction by John R. Lynch at Project Gutenberg

## HIRAM REVELS
http://www.biography.com/people/hiram-r-revels-9456129

John R. Lynch. "Chapter III", The Facts of Reconstruction

http://www.blackpast.org/aah/revels-hiram-rhoades-1827-1901

## ELIZABETH TAYLOR GREENFIELD
http://www.biography.com/people/elizabeth-taylor-greenfield-40267
http://www.blackpast.org/aah/greenfield-elizabeth-taylor-1819-1876
The Black Swan at Home and Abroad; A Biographical Sketch of Miss Elizabeth Taylor Greenfield, The American Vocalist. @ Gutenberg.org
RICHARD WRIGHT
Wright, Richard (1966). Black Boy. New York: Harper and Row Publishers. ISBN 0-06-083056-5.

Hazel Rowley, Richard Wright: The Life and Times, University of Chicago Press, 2001
http://www.biography.com/people/richard-wright-9537751

**WHARLEST JACKSON SR.**
http://nuweb9.neu.edu/civilrights/wharlest-jackson/

http://www.natchezdemocrat.com/2007/02/28/wharlest-
jackson-remembered/

http://www.jacksonfreepress.com/news/2005/oct/26/daddy-
get-up-this-son-of-natchez-wants-justice-too/

**PHILLIP WEST**
http://www.nbcnews.com/id/5676325/
Miss Lou Heritage Group and Tours Interview with Phillip
West on December 1, 2015

Made in the USA
Middletown, DE
02 October 2023